THE PREBUMPTIOUS MR. PUNCH
A play in two acts.

Published in 2014 by the Worcester Repertory Company.

© Peter Sutton 2013

Peter Sutton is hereby identified as the author of this work in accordance with Section 77 of the Copyright, Designs and Patents Act 1998.

This work remains the property of Peter Sutton. Rights to perform this production are obtainable from the Worcester Repertory Company by submitting an application in writing to:

Worcester Repertory Company
The Swan Theatre
The Moors
Worcester
WR1 3ED

info@worcester-rep.co.uk

Tel: 01905 726969
www.worcester-rep.co.uk

ABOUT THE WRITER

Peter Sutton began his playwriting career by submitting winning entries to local competitions, including an early version of *The Prebumptious Mr Punch*. In 2006 he wrote the one-man play *My Son Will* for an international Shakespeare Festival, and his play *Elgar and Alice* toured during the composer's anniversary celebrations in 2007 starring Gerald Harper. It was published in 2008 and revived at the Swan Theatre Worcester during the 2011 Three Choirs Festival. In 2012 he was commissioned to write a presentation on the life of the medieval poet William Langland for the Autumn in Malvern Festival. He has also appeared as an actor for the European Theatre Company, the Pascal Theatre Company, the Steam Industry and others, and he has played character parts on television and in small films.

In addition, he is an experienced linguist and researcher. He worked for seven years for Unesco, editing an international journal, overseeing other publications and heading a research project on prison education. He has translated numerous books and other documents from French, German and Spanish for international organisations, arts centres and lawyers, and he has written German language textbooks and academic articles and reports on education and languages. His translation of Langland's epic poem *Piers Plowman* into modern English verse has a publication date of 2015.

For more information see www.petersutton.eu

FROM THE WRITER

This play was inspired by seeing children laughing at the Punch and Judy puppet play. But what really happens these days to a man who beats his wife, mistreats his baby and batters to death anyone who gets up his not inconsiderable nose? He no longer faces the hangman but goes to prison, where the staff make comic attempts to reform him. Do they succeed? Of course they don't. That was the original basis for the play.

But then the characters complained, wanting to be taken more seriously. The custodial services, the medical team, the chaplaincy and the prison education staff all pointed out that they are more than figures of fun. They do their best against almost insuperable odds, and they deserve respect. Then Punch insisted on saying more about his background if we were going all serious on him, and Judy joined in, wanting to talk about her chaotic upbringing and her confused feelings for Punch. And finally the Policeman woke me up one morning and said he was not just a man with a truncheon and a helmet several sizes too small but a sentient and well-intentioned human being too, whose opinions should be listened to because they were based on first-hand experience. He suggested he should drop in to make sure Judy was all right while Punch was in prison.

This account may seem fanciful, but characters in plays do develop lives of their own, and authors need to accommodate them if they are to fit the story, and must allow them to take the action in the direction that suits them. Twelve years of searching for ways to achieve this harmony between characters and subject-matter led to a two-day workshop on the script directed by Svetlana Dimcovic and hosted by the Swan Theatre Worcester in 2011, and to a public reading at Actors and Writers London. Further ideas, particularly from a recalcitrant Punch who was still grumbling that he was made out to be a half-wit, led to another round of rewriting before the Worcester Repertory Company gave the finished play its first performance at the Swan in 2013.

Much of the original humour remains, but the play is now a more considered exploration of human relationships, the criminal justice system and the causes of violence. It has drawn throughout on my research into prison education and on my many encounters with prison staff and inmates in the UK and elsewhere, including the originals of Punch and the other characters, and it was enriched latterly by advice from the Worcestershire Forum Against Domestic Abuse and from theatre professionals. I hope that the end product is both truthful and funny. There is surely some of Punch in all of us.

worcester repertory company

First presented by the *Worcester Repertory Company* at the Swan Theatre Studio, 7th - 11th May 2013.

CAST

Punch	Andrew Rawle
Snipes, Policeman, Prison Governor, Warder, Chaplain and himself.	Rob Leetham
Judy, Judge, Jo the Clown, Doctor and herself.	Liz Grand

PRODUCTION

Director & Producer	Chris Jaeger
Lighting & Sound	Carl Maycroft
Stage Manager & Props	Gemma Martyn Smith
Costume	Isabelle Hunter
Video	JDA Media

THE PREBUMPTIOUS MR. PUNCH

by Peter Sutton

CHARACTERS & SETTING

The Policeman is Welsh, the Doctor North American.

The play is set in the present.

Costume changes should be minimal.

The set is a Punch and Judy fit-up which may open out to form the various locations.

The actors parallel the story of the play in their real lives.

They occasionally let the mask fall in Act 1, and they fully reveal their true selves and their relationships in Act 2. The names "Rob" and "Liz" should therefore be replaced by those of the actual performers.

The printed programme should make no mention of this conceit.

PROLOGUE

A Puppet Show in which the actors may take the parts of the Puppets.

PUPPET PUNCH: Hallo, boys and girls. I said, Hallo, boys and girls! Is there anybody there? I thought you'd all gone home. Let's try it one more time. Hallo, boys and girls! That's better. It's lovely to see you. And you've brought your grannies and granddads. Oh, it's your mummies and daddies, is it? It must be a trick of the light. Are you sitting bumfortably? Good, cos I'm going to sing you a little ditty. A witty ditty entitled "I may be a circus performer but they'll never make me swing from a rope."

PUPPET JUDY: (*off stage*) Punch!

PUPPET PUNCH: (*singing to the tune of The Man on the Flying Trapeze*) "He flies through the air and he misses the trees..."

PUPPET JUDY: (*off stage*) You'll wake the baby.

PUPPET PUNCH: "That clumsy baboon with the scabs on his knees..."

The BABY cries.

PUPPET JUDY: (*coming on with the BABY*) I said you'd wake the baby.

PUPPET PUNCH: Don't worry, Judy-pie. I'll sing her a loverly lullaby. You go and make the tea.

PUPPET JUDY: You make sure you look after her.

PUPPET PUNCH: I'll look after the Baby, Jude.

PUPPET JUDY: Will you call me, boys and girls, if he does anything nasty to the Baby? (*She waits for an audience reaction.*) Will you? You make sure you do. (*She goes off.*)

PUPPET PUNCH: (*tossing the BABY higher and higher*)
(*singing*) "Here we go round the Mulberry Bush,
The Mulberry Bush, the Mulberry Bush – "
Oh dear, I've dropped the baby.

PUPPET JUDY: (*coming back on*) What have you done, Punch? Where's our baby?

PUPPET PUNCH: I don't know. I expect the crocodile ate her.

PUPPET JUDY: You wicked old man, I shall go and fetch the Policeman.

PUPPET PUNCH: Go down and get him, and I'll give it him as well. (*He hits JUDY, who falls down inside the fit-up.*)
(*singing*) "Here we go round the Mulberry Bush,
The Mulberry Bush, the Mulberry Bush.
Here we go round the Mulberry Bush,
Where the booze all costs a fortune."

PUPPET POLICEMAN: (*coming on*) I'll teach you to wallop your wife, Mr Punch.

PUPPET PUNCH: (*hitting the POLICEMAN*) And I'll teach you to keep your nose out.

PUPPET POLICEMAN: You'll be made to suffer, Mr Punch.

PUPPET PUNCH: You're going to make my supper?

PUPPET POLICEMAN: I have a warrant to lock you up.

PUPPET PUNCH: And I have a warrant to knock you down. (*He hits the POLICEMAN, who falls down inside the fit-up.*) Ho ho, they'll never put me away and throw away the key. Not that professional prankster, the prebumptious Mr Punch!

The Prologue ends.

ACT ONE

"ROB" and "LIZ" come on. Throughout the Act they suggest through glances and occasional physical contact that they have just begun a relationship.

LIZ: Hallo, Boys and Girls. My name's [Liz] and I play Joey the Clown and the Judge and the Doctor. Oh, and Judy with her Baby.

ROB: And I'm [Rob] and I play everyone else: the Prison Governor, the Policeman and the Chaplain and the Warder. And Snipes with his dog Toby.

LIZ: And we're going to tell you the story of Mr Punch.

ROB: With the help of the old rascal himself, of course.

Punch does not appear.

With the help of the old rascal himself!

PUNCH comes on from an unexpected direction, into the bar of the Mulberry Bush Public House.

PUNCH: That's me. My name's Punch and I play...

ROB: Oh, for –.

LIZ: Punch!

PUNCH: (*to ROB*) What's the problem? I'm here, aren't I?

LIZ: But you – Oh!

ROB and LIZ go off and will become SNIPES and JUDY.

PUNCH: So, like I was saying, my name's Punch and I play – Punch. (*trying to work the pub jukebox*) No, it's an undertaker job.

(*singing the old song*)

"There is a tavern in the town, in the town.
The beer's like dog piss that's turned brown, that's turned brown…"

(*to the audience*)

All right, chief, are you? You want to chat her up, mate. Nice-looking bimbo like that. Well, not that marvellous, but you're not so fancy yourself. What you buggering about at out there?

ROB / SNIPES: (*off stage*) I'm seeing a dog about a man.

PUNCH: Cor dear, up his own arse, is our [Rob].

A dog barks.

Among others.

(*continuing the song*)
"I don't mind spit and sawdust on the ground,
It's in my beer it gets me down, gets me down."

SNIPES comes on.

SNIPES: Like a bit of music, don't you, Punch?

PUNCH: Got music in my soul, I have.

(*singing, to the Gilbert and Sullivan tune*)

"A wandering minstrel I,

A thing of shreds and patches,
I only know some snatches,
The record I've got is all scratches."

SNIPES: How's tricks?

PUNCH: Smashed the baby's brains out, walloped the missis.

SNIPES: Business as usual then, eh?

PUNCH: Pretty much. Bums up, madam. Or in your case, cod-face, down the hatch. Did you hear about this geezer who went to buy a dog? And the fellow said, my dog's got no…

SNIPES: We've heard it a million times.

PUNCH: No, this is different. My dog's got no tail, he says. That's a shame, says the geezer. Give him this. Why, says the fellow, what is it? A dog end, he says! A dog end!

SNIPES: Get them out of crackers, do you, Punch?

PUNCH: Kids love them. Give us a pint.

The dog barks.

(*singing*) "How much is that doggy in the window,
The one with the waggly tail?
He's already had fourteen lagers,
And now he's on spliffs and light ale."

SNIPES: Let's see your money, then.

PUNCH: What for?

SNIPES: The pint.

PUNCH: I haven't got any money.

SNIPES: You asked for it.

PUNCH: No, I didn't. I said, "Give us a pint."

The dog barks.

You want to do something about that dog.

SNIPES: He's only missing HMV. Come on, hand it over.

PUNCH: I tell you what. I'll look after the bar while you let him out. That's worth a pint.

SNIPES: Oh no. I know you.

PUNCH: Go on, Snipes. I've always fancied myself as a pumpkin.

SNIPES: A pumpkin?

PUNCH: A publican. With a round belly, a thick skin and a liking for departed spirits.

SNIPES: All right. But no cheating. The prices is all marked up.

SNIPES goes off. The dog barks excitedly.

PUNCH: Roll up, ladies and gents. Roll up, and see the great Mr Puncho do his world-famous impression of a publican. What's yours, my love? A wait wain? I'll go and get the cat to pee in a glass. And what are you having, Punch, my fine fellow? A glass of young and frisky? Thank you, Mr Punch. I don't mind if I do. And have one yourself. I will, Punch, that's very decent of you. Come on, laddies and bints, it's all doubles tonight. Plenty of time for seven deadly gins.

SNIPES comes back on.

That didn't take long.

SNIPES: He didn't want to go. Where did that whisky come from?

PUNCH: Out the Aristotle. Why? Do you want one?

SNIPES: That's a double.

PUNCH: Double, treble. What's the difference?

SNIPES: About two quid at time.

PUNCH: Leave off, Snipes. It's only money.

The dog barks.

You got him tied up again, have you?

SNIPES: What are you going to do about it?

PUNCH: I'd let him out again if I was you.

SNIPES: Not the dog. The money.

PUNCH: (*making to go off*) I know what. I'll sort him out for you.

SNIPES: He don't like strangers.

PUNCH: I'm good with dogs.

SNIPES: You said that about the hamster.

PUNCH goes off.

Pint of best, two double malts, that's – It's a lot, whatever it is.

PUNCH comes rushing on, holding the end of a string of sausages.

SNIPES: Oy, those are my bar snacks.

PUNCH: Let go, you three-ring flee circus.

PUNCH is drawn back off, as on a piece of elastic.

SNIPES: Punch, let go. Toby, drop them.

PUNCH comes on again pulling the sausages.

PUNCH: Give here, you sodden bathmat.

PUNCH is once more drawn off.

SNIPES: Leave him, Punch. He'll have your nuts off.

The sound of growling, barking and crashing of furniture, ending in a yelp and a whimper.

What's going on? Punch?

PUNCH returns carrying a mangled half string of sausages.

Made a great success of that, didn't you?

PUNCH: I shut him up for you.

SNIPES: He already was.

PUNCH: Not like now.

SNIPES looks at PUNCH and hurries off. PUNCH takes another drink.

Did you hear the one about the orange that thought it was a grapefruit? It must have been pithed at the time.

SNIPES comes back on.

SNIPES: You've bloody killed him, that's what you've done.

PUNCH: Like I said. I shut him up.

SNIPES: You've killed my Tobes.

PUNCH: Oy, oy, do I smell a doggy smell?

SNIPES: Come on, put 'em up.

PUNCH: Read all about it. Scandal of landlord's secret life.

SNIPES: Put 'em up, damn you.

PUNCH: Back off, Swipes.

SNIPES: (*dancing around, tapping at the air*) I'll give you Swipes. Heugh! Heugh!

PUNCH: Let me finish my pint, will you?

SNIPES: Come on, you yellow-belly. Bantam weight champion I was down the boys' club. Heugh! Heugh! What do you make of that? Eh? Come on, put down that beer and fight me like a man. Take that! And that. That's the way to do it.

PUNCH hits SNIPES hard.

PUNCH: No. That is.

SNIPES: Oh, you – !

SNIPES drops dead. The actor is genuinely hurt, and lies still.

PUNCH: You want to sting like a bee, not ponce about like a butterfly. Help yourselves, larigs and yobs. Everything's on the house tonight. (*taking money from the till*) Nearly forgot my wages. (*to the audience*) I did look after the bar. (*He considers taking the sausages.*) No they're all chewed.

As PUNCH leaves the pub he kicks the jukebox, which finally starts.

Hey, Jude!

JUDY: (*off stage*) What?

PUNCH: Get your big fat bazookas out here.

JUDY comes on with the Baby.

JUDY / LIZ: Why? What is it? (*looking at SNIPES / ROB, speaking as LIZ*) Oh. my God.

PUNCH: We're going out on the town, that's what.

LIZ: (*examining ROB*) We can't.

PUNCH: Leave him.

LIZ: But he's out cold. You've...

PUNCH: Oodles of dosh, that's what we've got. Oodles and boodles and spoodles of dosh.

ROB stirs.

LIZ: (*to ROB*) Are you all right?

ROB: I'll live.

PUNCH: Where did I get the spondulicks, you enquire? How nice of you to ask. I went round with the hat. "Spare us the price of a cuppa, my old china. Born with this hump, I was."

ROB: You can say that again.

LIZ: Are you sure you're okay?

ROB: Yeah, yeah.

ROB goes off. He will become the POLICEMAN.

PUNCH: Because I am the cleverest, cudddliest – what am I?

LIZ / JUDY: You are the cleverest, cuddliest, crookedest man that ever there was.

PUNCH: I am indeed. And you are the crookedest woman.

PUNCH dances around, singing to the tune of the Blue Danube and tossing the Baby in the air and back and forth with JUDY.

"Oh, we'll have a nosh in somewhere posh,
Where you'll make a splosh in~your mackintosh.
The stuffies with dosh will say Oh gosh,
Those slobs are both sloshed and they don't wash…"

There is a knock at the door.

Well, well. Here is the great Henry Irving again.

"We shall cosh, we shall squash

Any tosh who talks such josh…"

The knocking continues.

You never sent for the Old Bill, did you, Jude?

JUDY: No.

PUNCH: Neither did I. Sod off!

(*singing, to the tune of "The Man who Broke the Bank at Montecarlo"*)

"As he strolls along by Clapton Pond…"

JUDY: Aren't you going to answer it?

PUNCH: No. We're out, didn't I tell you?
"…With his nose stuck in the air,
You will see the hookers stare…"

POLICEMAN: (*off stage*) Mr Punch?

PUNCH opens the door an inch and closes it again.

PUNCH: Not today, thank you.

JUDY: Was it the fuzz?

PUNCH: Jehovah's Witness.

JUDY: How did he know your name?

PUNCH: Jehovah must have told him. (*tossing the Baby to JUDY*) If anyone wants me, I'm in China.

PUNCH goes off.

JUDY: Oh look, Baby, you've been sick all down your front again. I wonder how that happened.

POLICEMAN: Open up. We know you're in there.

JUDY: It's mess all the time with you, isn't it, Baby? Mess and stress and sick down your dress.

POLICEMAN: Do you want us to break the door down?

JUDY: No, I don't. Stupid question.

The knocking becomes fiercer.

All right. Keep your helmet on.

JUDY opens the door. The POLICEMAN comes in.

(*speaking as LIZ to ROB*) Are you really okay?

ROB / POLICEMAN: Yeah, no thanks to that prat. (*speaking as the POLICEMAN*) Mr Punch, I am arrest... Where's he gone then, my love?

JUDY: China.

POLICEMAN: Take the bus, did he?

JUDY: I expect he's gone on his bike.

POLICEMAN: In which case the pandas will get him. You're Mrs Punch, are you?

JUDY: That depends.

POLICEMAN: If you are, I'm sorry to say he'll be going down for a long one.

JUDY: And if I'm not?

POLICEMAN: I'm a good deal less sorry. Pooh, that baby smells.

PUNCH comes back on.

PUNCH: Would you believe it, the backyard's buzzing with bluebottles.

POLICEMAN: Mr Punch, I am arresting...

PUNCH: Oh blimey, there's one in here and all.

POLICEMAN: Mr Punch, I am arresting you for doing in the landlord of the Mulberry Bush public house, Mr Henry Snipes.

PUNCH: (*quoting SNIPES*) "Bantam weight champion I was down the boys' club. Heugh! Heugh!"

POLICEMAN: Not to mention causing suffering to his dog.

PUNCH: It didn't suffer a bit.

POLICEMAN: You do not have to say anything...

PUNCH: Not for long.

POLICEMAN: ...but it may harm your defence if you fail to put the right man in goal, and anything you do say is likely to be kicked into touch. Come on, let's be having you.

The POLICEMAN marches PUNCH to his cell. JUDY becomes the JUDGE, and the POLICEMAN will become the PRISON GOVERNOR.

PUNCH: And that, dailies and temps, I kid you not, is exactly how it was.

(*singing, continuing Montecarlo*)

"You will see the hookers stare,
'He must be a zillionnaire.'
You can hear them whistle and shout out 'Hi!'
You can see them think, it's worth a try…"

JUDGE: Mr Punch!

PUNCH: (*singing*) "He's the man that robbed the bank at Hackney Marshes."

JUDGE: Mr Punch!!

PUNCH: What?

JUDGE: Pay attention when I'm talking to you.

PUNCH: Why?

JUDGE: Because you're in a court of law.

PUNCH: I was in my own front room a moment ago.

JUDGE: You're not now.

PUNCH: And you were Jude.

JUDGE: Well, now I'm the Judge.

PUNCH: (*to the audience*) Isn't the magic of theatre amazing?

JUDGE: Have you anything to say before I pass sentence?

PUNCH: How about, I was off my head?

JUDGE: If you're sane enough to plead insanity, you're sane enough to be sentenced.

PUNCH: I knew there'd be a catch.

JUDGE: You have killed a man. And his dog.

PUNCH: No, I haven't.

JUDGE: Yes, you have.

PUNCH: Not the dog: Snipes. The old bugger died of a heart attack.

JUDGE: Which is why you're not up for murder.

PUNCH: Then what the hell am I doing here?

JUDGE: You're here because you hit him. And in view of your previous record of violence…

PUNCH: What violence?

JUDGE: Breach of the peace, criminal damage, obstructing the highway, threatening behaviour, affray, trespass, and committing a public nuisance. Not to mention assaults on prison officers.

PUNCH: Nothing violent there. Is there, burgers and grills?

JUDGE: I am going to give you five years for causing actual bodily harm. Plus two years concurrently for causing suffering to an animal.

PUNCH: It had jaws like a man-trap and teeth like pitchforks.

JUDGE: So have I. Take him down.

PUNCH: That won't do any good.

JUDGE: Maybe not to you, but the rest of us will enjoy it immensely.

PUNCH: (*referring to the two actors ROB and LIZ*) I'll bet you will. The smart-arse pair of you.

The JUDGE goes off and becomes JO.

(*singing, to the tune of "I do like to be beside the seaside"*)

"Oh, I do like to be inside, not outside
Cos inside is nice as nice can be.
 I do like to stroll along the Prom, Prom, Prom
With my slop pail full of tiddly om pom pom..."

JO and the GOVERNOR come on.

I told you this should have been a musical.

JO: What are we going to do with him, Governor?

GOVERNOR: The same as usual. Strip-search him once a week for drugs, teach him motor mechanics and hope he finds God.

PUNCH: You still sound like Snipes.

LIZ: No, he doesn't.

PUNCH: (*as if ROB*) "How shall I play him, I wonder? As a hex-harmy hofficer with bullets for brains or as a soft touch who sucks up to crims?"

LIZ: You concentrate on playing yourself.

PUNCH: I will if you will.

GOVERNOR: You must know the routine by now, Mr Punch.

PUNCH: Yes, Guv'nor, sir. Three meals a day, compulsory exercise, and twenty hours out of twenty-four to stare at the ceiling.

GOVERNOR: Got it in a nutshell.

PUNCH: No drink, no dope and no dipping my wick.

GOVERNOR: Spot on.

PUNCH: Thanks to you.

LIZ: Shut up.

GOVERNOR: The Prison Chaplain will look after your welfare…

PUNCH: A hundred quid a week and he can leave me in peace.

GOVERNOR: Not that kind of welfare, I'm afraid. Your physical and mental health will be checked by a medic. And you may write and receive one letter a week.

PUNCH: That's a fat lot of good to me.

JO: In which case we should be able to help you.

PUNCH: Some kind of miracle-worker, are you?

GOVERNOR: This lady is an education officer.

PUNCH: Can't be then, can she?

JO: Lots of people need help with reading and writing.

PUNCH: Only if they're thick.

JO: For all sorts of reasons. They may have missed out on schooling…

PUNCH: What's that?

JO: Exactly. They may have problems at home, or trouble with eyesight or hearing, or they may not be able to identify the shapes of the letters themselves…

PUNCH: You can't tell T from P in here.

JO: That's why I work here. To give them another shot at it, because it's important to keep up family ties.

PUNCH: In my family we never wore ties. Didn't you get it, T from P?

GOVERNOR: It's the oldest joke in the place. You will also be entitled to a visit once a month from your wife.

PUNCH: Any sex go with that?

GOVERNOR: We don't have the facilities.

PUNCH: I do.

GOVERNOR: We'll give you something for that. Now, you remember what is meant by sentence planning?

PUNCH: Think before I speak?

JO: No, but it's not a bad idea.

GOVERNOR: The point of sentence planning is to get you a job when you go back out.

PUNCH: I had a job once. Stuck inside this giant orange ball by a bin of drinks in a supermarket. "Hallo sonny, have a puke-pack."

GOVERNOR: Ah. Merchandising.

PUNCH: Agonizing. I was pissing pips for a week.

JO: Not all jobs are like that.

PUNCH: Such as yours, eh? Being paid peanuts to teach us monkeys?

JO: I don't do this all the time.

PUNCH: What else do you do? Sit at some desk, do you? Watching the clock, asking permission to go for a pee?

JO: No, I'm a street performer.

PUNCH: Get away.

JO: Tightrope-walking, clowning, that kind of thing.

PUNCH: I thought you meant you were on the game.

JO: Well, I didn't.

PUNCH: I've always fancied myself as a circus act. Roll up, roll up. Watch the mighty, the marvellous, the magnificent Mr Puncho. He packs the power of a pachyderm, with a hump and a stick that'll make you squirm.

GOVERNOR: I'll put you down for the woodwork shop.

PUNCH: I thought you might.

JO and the GOVERNOR go off and become JUDY and the POLICEMAN again.

(singing, continuing "I do like to be beside the seaside")

"So if you will come inside beside me
You'll be beside yourself with glee.
There are lots of shits outside
I would love to see inside.
Inside not outside,
Instead of me."

PUNCH goes off.

JUDY is at home, heating milk for the Baby's bottle and drinking gin. Loud pop music is playing. There is a knock at the door.

JUDY: *(shouting)* Go away.

More knocking.

POLICEMAN: *(off stage)* Are you all right?

JUDY: "Are you all right?"

More knocking

POLICEMAN: I'm catching my death standing out here.

JUDY: Good.

POLICEMAN: Come on now. I'm not really a Jehovah's Witness.

JUDY: (*opening the door*) You might be.

The POLICEMAN comes in.

Come to warm your handcuffs, have you, Mr Plod?

POLICEMAN: I came about the baby.

JUDY: What baby?

POLICEMAN: The baby that lives here, poor mite.

He turns off the music.

That's better.

JUDY: That's nice, I must say. Barging your way into other people's houses and turning off the music they're listening to.

POLICEMAN: I couldn't hear myself think.

JUDY: What does that sound like?

POLICEMAN: What?

JUDY: You thinking?

POLICEMAN: Had a bit to drink, have we, my love?

JUDY: (*turning the radio back on*) We like our music. Don't we, Baby?

POLICEMAN: (*turning the radio off again*) It can damage your hearing if it's that loud.

The Baby cries.

JUDY: Now see what you've done.

POLICEMAN: It's the noise, that's what upset him.

JUDY: Her.

POLICEMAN: Her what?

JUDY: The Baby's a her.

POLICEMAN: In my game all babies are male until proved otherwise.

JUDY: You're in the wrong game then, mister.

POLICEMAN: Look, let me check that the Baby's all right and you can deafen yourselves to your heart's content.

JUDY: What did you have to arrest him for, that's what I want to know.

POLICEMAN: What did you expect me to do? Congratulate him? Hm, she looks all right.

JUDY: (*picking up the Baby and nearly dropping her*) I told you she was all right. I'm all right, she's all right, we're all all right.

POLICEMAN: Give her to me. And sit down before you fall down. Pooh, this baby smells again.

JUDY: Why did you arrest my belovely Punch?

POLICEMAN: Your belovely Punch was a murder waiting to happen since he could lift half a brick.

JUDY: It's not our fault if people leave bricks lying around.

POLICEMAN: Oh yes, the usual sob story. I never had a chance. My dad ran off with a mermaid and my mam was out fishing for punters whenever I came home.

JUDY: My dad did. And my mum was. Which is why I stayed at home. Cos we were going to give our Baby a chance, me and Punchy. And now she hasn't got a chance and I shall have to work my knickers off like my mum and be brought home by a man in a van and she'll be like me and it's not our fault and life's not fair. And I don't know what to do.

POLICEMAN: You could change the baby for a start.

JUDY: I'm not changing my baby for anyone. And I'm not changing Punchy either. I love my baby and I love my Punchy and Punchy loves me and I need a wee.

POLICEMAN: Then you go and – Oh hell, the milk's boiling over now. (*seeing JUDY waving the gin bottle*) Give me that!

JUDY: Not too much, gin's not good for her.

POLICEMAN: You're never giving her gin?

JUDY: That's why I said not too much.

POLICEMAN: Sometimes I wonder why I do this job.

JUDY: So do I. Ooh, ooh, stay up, wee. Hoo, hah. Stay up, wee. Hooooooooh.

JUDY goes off hopping.

POLICEMAN: (*emptying the gin bottle*) We'd better get rid of this stuff while your mammy's out of the way, hadn't we, Baby? She didn't really mean me to give you gin. It was just the demon in the bottle talking. The djinn, I suppose you might say. The djinn in the bottle. Djinn like genie, see. In the bot–. I'd have trained as a social worker if I'd wanted to be one. (*He tests the baby's bottle against his cheek.*) Right. Now, don't you dare spill as much as one tiniest, weeniest infinitesimalest little droplet. I am not arriving at the nick smelling of milky baby. (*He starts feeding the Baby.*)

(*singing, to the Gilbert and Sullivan tune*)

"With constabulary duties to be done, to be done,
A policeman's lot is not a nappy one, nappy one."

Oh Duw!

JUDY comes back on and snatches the Baby.

JUDY: Give her here, you sodding baby-snatcher!

POLICEMAN: You asked me to feed her.

JUDY: Oh no, I didn't.

POLICEMAN: Oh yes, you did.

JUDY: Didn't.

POLICEMAN: Did. You did. You did, you did, you did.

JUDY: You been in panto, have you, Mr Plod?

POLICEMAN: Star of the local am dram, I was once. And my name's Owen actually.

JUDY: Don't know much about babies, though. Do you, Mr Acherly?

POLICEMAN: I do, because my mother was a health visitor. She took me with her when I was a tiddler.

JUDY: Is that what you came for? To tell me your mother was a health visitor, or that you were a fish?

POLICEMAN: Community policing, they call it.

JUDY: I think I must go and lie down.

POLICEMAN: And I must get back to the station.

JUDY: What time's your train?

POLICEMAN: Police sta– Oh sod it, Baby. If I lived with your mammy, I'd be on the gin.

JUDY: What's wrong with that?

POLICEMAN: Nothing, I er – oh, lor', I – I'll look in again if I'm passing.

The POLICEMAN / ROB and JUDY / LIZ touch briefly before ROB goes off. He will become the WARDER.

JUDY: You needn't bother. We're all right as we are. Aren't we, Baby?

JUDY picks up the Baby and goes off, walking into the furniture.

Oh, bum!

PUNCH is in his cell. JUDY becomes JO.

PUNCH: How are you today, Wall? Yeah, I know. It eats into you, doesn't it? Gets right into your footings. But here comes a circus act that'll cheer us up: the Three Rs – reading, rithmetic and right on your tits.

(*singing, to the tune of "Row, row. row your boat"*)

"In, out, in and out, every inmate's dream.
Dribbly, dribbly, dribbly, dribbly, screw Miss Peaches and Cream."

JO comes on. PUNCH goes on "rowing".

JO: Let's get started on your assessment.

PUNCH: What do they call you?

JO: You can call me Jo.

PUNCH: Joey the Clown?

JO: Just Jo. Could you stop doing that, do you think?

PUNCH: What about this tightrope-walking, then?

JO: It's a skill I picked up along the way.

PUNCH: Then you can teach it to me.

JO: I'd rather stick to arithmetic.

PUNCH: What does two and two make?

JO: What do you think?

PUNCH: Five usually.

JO: It does with some people. If I have nine cakes and I give away seven, how many do I have left?

PUNCH: That depends how hungry I am.

JO: Let's suppose I'm not.

PUNCH: Then you and I can have one each.

JO: Good. And if I buy another three, what does that make altogether?

PUNCH: Three.

JO: What?

PUNCH: We ate the other two.

JO: I think we can tick the arithmetic box. Don't you?

PUNCH: Why don't you and me do a double act? Puncho and Jo head over heels on the high wire.

JO: Just look at this reading sheet, will you? Do you recognise any of the letters?

PUNCH: What letters?

JO: Maybe we'd better start from the beginning.

PUNCH: People are always saying that to me.

JO: I can't think why. The middle one is 'a'.[1]

PUNCH: a. a, a, a, a, a.

JO: Good. And this is b.

---

1 'a' as in 'cat', not ABC.

PUNCH: b.

JO: Yes. And this last one is – ?

PUNCH: Another b.

JO: No, d.

PUNCH: Oh, I get it.

JO: I thought you would.

PUNCH: One faces this way and one faces that.

JO: That's right. And what does it say when we put them together?

PUNCH: I don't know.

JO: Yes, you do.

PUNCH: Not until we've ticked the reading box.

JO: Bad.

PUNCH: Correct.

JO: And this is – ?

PUNCH: Bab.

JO: Near enough. And if we put the two words together – ?

PUNCH: Dab bab?

JO: And if you look at things the right way round for a change you get – ?

PUNCH: You're taking the piss.

JO: You get bad dad, don't you?

PUNCH: I know you do. That's why you're taking the piss.

JO: No, I'm not.

PUNCH: Yes, you are. You're saying I'm a bad dad.

JO: I'm not.

PUNCH: Don't tell lies, Jo.

JO: Why did you tell us you couldn't write letters?

PUNCH: I didn't.

JO: But you didn't miss out on schooling?

PUNCH: Yes, I did. I was short-sighted.

JO: And the dog ate your homework?

PUNCH: It's true. They sat me at the back because I was ugly. I couldn't see the board.

JO: I think what happened was probably more like this. The teacher was explaining six times nine or where America is or something but you wanted to know about other things instead: what the moon is made of or why men have moustaches. So the teacher got cross and told you to sit at the back and be quiet. Is that how it was?

PUNCH: No.

JO: Then what was it like?

PUNCH: I don't know. I wasn't listening.

JO: Look at the sheet again, will you?

PUNCH: I can't.

JO: Why not?

PUNCH: Because I've got to dig the Governor's garden. (*producing a list*) See what he wants? "Big debs."

JO: You're sure it's not dig beds?

PUNCH: Positive. "Prune jasminum nudiflorum. Plant out da..." What's this? Dabliabs?

JO: Dahlias.

PUNCH: So it is. How many Hs in dahlias?

JO: One.

PUNCH: Thought so. And now we've ticked another stupid fucking box you can teach me something useful like tightrope-walking.

JO: I'll have to see what I can do.

PUNCH: Hear that, Puncho? The big top beckons.

JO: But only if you stop winding us up. (*holding out a book*) And in the meantime, since you're so fond of playing with words, you might like this.

PUNCH: What is it? A dictionary?

JO: A book of verse. My Hundred Best Poems.

PUNCH: Poems?

JO: Yes.

PUNCH: There are two sorts of people in the world, Jo. One does things, and the other reads about them.

(opening the poetry book and reading badly)

"In Ksanadu did cub-lay can
A stately pleasure dome decree,
Where 'alf the sacred river ran
Through..."

What's that about? Haven't the faintest, Mr P.

JO: "In Xanadu did Kubla Khan
A stately pleasure-dome decree,
Where Alph the sacred river ran..."

PUNCH: Know it, do you?

JO: I learnt it at school.

PUNCH: You can't have gone to the same one as me.

JO: Probably not.

JO goes off and becomes JUDY once more.

PUNCH: Shall I tell you why the Punch has got a hump? It's because of all the crap that's been piled on his back by poetry-punters like you from the "other school". Don't tread on the grass, don't drop litter, don't hide in the toilet when the ticket collector comes, don't vault over the barriers, don't break the speed limit, don't pinch the milk off the doorstep, don't run after my daughter, don't have noisy parties, don't swear, don't smoke, don't take dope, don't drink, don't breathe, don't live, and don't get up the snouts of pig's runts like me! (*shouting after JO*) And I am *not* a bad dad. In fact I'd be a bloody good dad if you let me.

JUDY comes in. The WARDER stands to one side.

JUDY: Are you moaning again?

PUNCH: That's nice, isn't it? What about "How are you?" or "Lovely to see you, man of my dreams"?

JUDY: Don't take it out on me, Punch.

PUNCH: You've got to take it out on someone in this yodeller's paradise.

JUDY: You wouldn't be in here if you hadn't hit Snipes so hard.

PUNCH: What's the point of hitting people softly?

JUDY: They don't fall over and die. How are you getting on with the woodwork?

PUNCH: I've been learning planing.

JUDY: I thought they were made of metal these days.

PUNCH: And there was Joey the Clown making me think women have brains.

JUDY: How *are* you getting on?

PUNCH: They started me off with a bit of wood and told me to shave it till the edge was smooth.

JUDY: What are you going to make?

PUNCH: Nothing.

JUDY: Why not?

PUNCH: When it got too thin they threw it away. They put me in the laundry after that.

JUDY: What happened?

PUNCH: Two broken ankles, three cracked hips and a flood in the basement.

JUDY: (*sympathetically*) Owoh, Punchy.

PUNCH: What have I ever been good at? Except getting myself banged up?

JUDY: You took care of me and Baby.

PUNCH: Did I?

JUDY: You stayed. Which is more than my dad did when I was born.

PUNCH: Of course I stayed. I love my Baby-boo.

JUDY: We both do.

PUNCH: Why didn't you bring her this time?

JUDY: She's all right.

PUNCH: You've never left her sitting on the pot again?

JUDY: No, I left her with a bottle.

PUNCH: Guinness?

JUDY: They'd run out, so it had to be Murphy's.

PUNCH: Eh?

JUDY: Don't be dafter than you have to, Punch. I left her with the neighbours.

PUNCH: It's the sort of half-arsed thing you would do.

JUDY: It's the sort of half-arsed thing we did do.

PUNCH: That's not my fault.

JUDY: No. Ginny the Pinny says it's your upbringing.

PUNCH: Ginny the what?

JUDY: The health visitor.

PUNCH: What do we want a health visitor for?

JUDY: For Baby. She tells me things I don't know.

PUNCH: Says a lot then, does she?

JUDY: I can't help not knowing things, any more than you can.

WARDER: Time!

PUNCH: Last orders if you please.

JUDY: I'm going to look after our baby, Punch.

PUNCH: I was going to look after her before they put me in here.

WARDER: Come on boys and girls. Break it up!

The WARDER goes off and becomes the GOVERNOR.

PUNCH: Bring her next time.

JUDY: I will. See you, fruity-pie.

PUNCH: I miss you, Bumcious.

JUDY: I miss you too, Giggle-stick.

PUNCH: Jelly-belly.

JUDY: Humpy.

PUNCH: Love you, Mrs Tittymouse.

JUDY: Come to think of it, it was that policeman got me the health visitor.

PUNCH: What policeman?

JUDY: The one that got me the – the nice one.

PUNCH: Nice one!

JUDY: Yes. You'd remember him.

PUNCH: Why?

JUDY: Cos he's the one that arrested you.

JUDY goes off and becomes JO.

PUNCH: "The one that arr – " Jude, what you – ?
There was a nice plod from Tredegar
Who arrested me cos he was eager.
Well, thank you a bunch
For banging up Punch.
When I'm out your chances are meagre.

The GOVERNOR comes on.

GOVERNOR: Ah, a limerick.

PUNCH: (*looking at a plant*) Is it? I thought it was a sibannac.

GOVERNOR: A what?

PUNCH: (*to the audience*) Back-slang for cannabis.

GOVERNOR: The garden's keeping you busy then?

PUNCH: Oh yes, we've got it all in here, Guv'nor. Creepers, grasses, beds full of pansies.

GOVERNOR: How long have you had the raspberries?

PUNCH: Long as I can remember. Oh, them. The last bloke put them in, before he got let out for being innocent.

JO comes on.

JO: Still a laugh a minute, aren't you?

PUNCH: Laughter makes the world go round. Or in some cases, pear-shaped. Do you know what would look good up against that wall?

GOVERNOR: A climber, at a guess.

PUNCH: You've heard it before, haven't you?

JO: Right, up you go, Punch.

PUNCH: Up where?

JO: *(pointing upwards)* Up the greasy pole.

PUNCH: You mean – ?

JO: Yes. Tightrope-walking.

PUNCH: Oh, great. Did you hear about the deaf prison governor and the great escape plan?

GOVERNOR: No.

PUNCH: Neither did he.

PUNCH goes off to perform his tightrope-walking act. (His place could be taken by a puppet.) PUNCH's voice comes from off-stage.

JO: You get yourself clipped on. And then you need to keep going nice and steadily. If you fall off, the harness will stop you. All right?

PUNCH: Didn't I tell you I was afraid of heights?

JO: No, because you aren't.

GOVERNOR: You reckon acrobatics is the answer, do you, Jo?

JO: Have you got a better idea, Governor?

GOVERNOR: In Punch's case – no.

PUNCH: Neither have I.

JO: You keep quiet and collect your thoughts. Are you clipped on? Good. Off you go. Remember, each step is a moment in time. There's no hurry, you've all day if you need it.

PUNCH: I've five years if I need it.

JO: So take it gently. Feel the rope with the sole of your foot. That's it, look straight ahead, not at me. Excellent. You're doing brilliantly.

PUNCH: You'll never guess what I can see from up here.

GOVERNOR: What?

PUNCH: In the Chaplain's office. He's bonking Doctor Nightinjail.

JO: He's not!

PUNCH: (*referring to ROB and LIZ*) Oh yes, he is.
(*singing, to the tune of Just a Song at Twilight*)
"Just a thong at twilight
When the tights are low…"
I nearly went arse over tit!

JO: Look where you're going! Slowly. That's better.

PUNCH: (*singing, to the tune of the First World War song*)
"There's a long, long trail a-winding…"
Warrawagh!

JO: Gently! I want to see you get to the end.

PUNCH: So do I.
"Into the land of my dreams…"

JO: That's it. It's only a few more steps.

PUNCH: "Where Miss Nightinjail is bringing..."

JO: Two more...

PUNCH: "Me her pink custard creams."

JO: One more.

PUNCH: (*success*) Hahahay!

JO: There, magnificent. You've done it. That was tremendous. I told you you could do it. Bravo for Mr Punch!

PUNCH: Bravo for Joey the Clown.

GOVERNOR: And the idiot at the Home Office who let us do it.

JO: Unclip yourself, Punch, and I'll see you back at the Unit.

GOVERNOR: But you realise we shall be laughing stocks if this wheeze goes belly up?

JO: As far as Punch is concerned, we already are.

ROB: (*touching LIZ affectionately*) Let's hope so.

The GOVERNOR / ROB and JO / LIZ go off. They will become the POLICEMAN and JUDY.

PUNCH comes on.

PUNCH: (*reciting*) "In Ksanadu did Cupcake Stan
A stately pleasure dome decree,
Where Alf the shady spivver ran
A timeshare scam with his mate Dan
Down by the sunbed sea..."

Oh. The turtle doves have flown. Have you ever had the feeling you're talking to yourself, Punch? Frequently, Mr Punch.

PUNCH goes off.

JUDY and the POLICEMAN come on, into JUDY's house. The Baby is in a cot.

POLICEMAN: (*refilling his glass with sherry*) Off the gin then, are you?

JUDY: Yes. I worked it out. If gin costs twice as much as sherry but only gets me half as drunk again, it's cheaper to buy the sherry.

POLICEMAN: I can see that. It's only logical.

JUDY: Go on. Fill it up.

POLICEMAN: No, that'll do. You've got to give it space to breathe.

JUDY: Like me.

POLICEMAN: Like all of us.

JUDY: I never had space before you came on the scene.

POLICEMAN: Punch was always on top of you? If you know what I mean.

JUDY: Everything was.

POLICEMAN: He never – hurt you, did he?

JUDY: No.

POLICEMAN: There are things we can do if he did.

JUDY: He didn't.

POLICEMAN: Are you sure?

JUDY: Yes. No more than – . If he gave me a slap it was my fault. Not like –.

POLICEMAN: What?

JUDY: That was ages ago. It doesn't matter any more.

POLICEMAN: Yes, it does.

JUDY: It's nothing.

POLICEMAN: It must be something.

JUDY: Well like I said, my mother wasn't there mostly when I got home.

POLICEMAN: Ah. Your dad.

JUDY: Yes.

POLICEMAN: The one who ran off with the mermaid?

JUDY: No, the one I called Dad.

POLICEMAN: The man in the van?

JUDY: That was someone else. He lived with us for a bit too. No, I mean my Dad dad…

POLICEMAN: Even though he wasn't really?

JUDY: Yes. Well, he wasn't around the whole time either. But he was more than the other one or the real one. I always knew when he was coming cos my mum would get all dressed up. And then they'd go out, and when they came home he'd slap me on the bum or squeeze my tits. Friendly-like, he said, but it wasn't really.

POLICEMAN: It never is.

JUDY: And next morning there'd be toilet paper all over the bathroom where my mum had wiped off the make-up and missed the bowl and – well sometimes she was so pissed she walked into the doorpost. And once, well once she puked all over the bed so bad after they'd had a night out that my dad had to come into my room – at least that's what he said.

POLICEMAN: I might have known.

JUDY: And after that he, well when I got back from school he was there sometimes.

POLICEMAN: It makes me mad when I hear that kind of thing.

JUDY: It didn't matter too much because by then I knew what was what.

POLICEMAN: Of course it mattered.

JUDY: Sorry.

POLICEMAN: For what, for goodness' sake?

JUDY: I'm sorry if it bothers you.

POLICEMAN: It doesn't. Not how you think.

JUDY: I suppose I ought to have done something.

POLICEMAN: Your mother certainly ought to have done something.

JUDY: She couldn't open a tin, hardly.

POLICEMAN: "Ho, ho, what a laugh, I got my end away with a twelve-year-old!"

JUDY: Thirteen.

POLICEMAN: Same difference. Oh, I'm not blaming you. I'm not blaming him really. It's family history. Usually too little family and too much history. In the old days, see, people who broke the rules were given a clip round the ear by the bobby on the beat, and then their mam or their dad did the same. That's how they learnt right and wrong before it was too late. Not any more. Nobody teaches them the difference, and when they do get caught, they have more opportunities than I had outside. It's all prisoners' welfare and psychological tests and developing your full potential. And all they do is thumb their noses.

JUDY: My dad wasn't caught.

POLICEMAN: More's the pity. It's very frustrating, being in the law and order business.

JUDY: Is that why you call in here?

POLICEMAN: They don't understand me at the station like you do.

JUDY: You do sound down in the dumps today.

POLICEMAN: To tell you the truth, I'm not going in today. Or ever again.

JUDY: You mean you've left the police?

POLICEMAN: I have.

JUDY: Why?

POLICEMAN: They found out I'd been dropping in here.

JUDY: What's wrong with that?

POLICEMAN: It's frowned on, see. Relationships with the wives of the people you put in chokey.

JUDY: I didn't know we had a relationship.

POLICEMAN: Abuse of my position, they called it. Unprofessional, like.

JUDY: That's silly.

POLICEMAN: I can see their point of view. It's rules again, see. We all have to abide by rules.

JUDY: That's what Punch always said. As long as it was his rules.

POLICEMAN: I don't mind really because I'd been thinking of doing something else for a while.

JUDY: What?

POLICEMAN: No, I couldn't, I…

JUDY: What?

POLICEMAN: You'd laugh.

JUDY: No, I wouldn't.

POLICEMAN: Well, I've – I've got a yen to go back on the stage.

JUDY: The stage?

POLICEMAN: Professionally, like.

JUDY: I'd have a fit if I had to stand up in front of all those people.

POLICEMAN: Not acting. But I have these puppets at home, and I do shows for kids in my spare time. Orphanages, schools, that kind of thing. Marvellous it is, to hear them giggling away.

JUDY: Puppets?

POLICEMAN: The Woodentops, I call them. A boy and girl who everyone thinks are stupid, but they always win in the end.

JUDY: Blow me.

POLICEMAN: Didn't know I was a star of stage, screen and birthday parties, did you?

JUDY: No.

POLICEMAN: They think I'm barmy at the station, but if everyone who was barmy was put away, one half of the population would have to lock up the other half. And that would never do, would it?

JUDY: Do you know what I've always wanted to do?

POLICEMAN: Tell me.

JUDY: Work in a clothes shop. With models in the windows that I can dress, like dolls. But it was chippies and a bookie where I lived. So I never did.

POLICEMAN: You might one day.

JUDY: Not till Baby's gone to school. And anyway I – well, school and me never sort of got on.

The Baby wails.

Come on, young lady, it's no good having a daddy-paddy. It's time you were in the land of nod. Oh, Mr Plod, did you hear that? Land of nod!

POLICEMAN: If I had a penny for every time you've made a joke about nods and plods – .

JUDY: How about one for the road?

POLICEMAN: No, I'd better be going. It's not much longer, Judy, my love, till – . You just keep on hanging in there.

JUDY: We will, won't we, Baby?

POLICEMAN: You do that. And thanks for the sherry and the – toad in the hole.

JUDY: My pleasure.

POLICEMAN: It sounds a bit rude, doesn't it?

JUDY: Does it, Owen?

POLICEMAN: Yes, well, I'll er –.

JUDY: I expect you will. Oh look, she's gone to sleep.

The POLICEMAN and JUDY go off, perhaps heading for the bedroom. They will become the DOCTOR and the CHAPLAIN. PUNCH comes on.

PUNCH: (*singing, to the tune of "What shall we do with the drunken sailor?"*)
"What shall we do with the blue-arsed plonker,
What shall we do with the two-faced bonker,
What shall we do with the lying stonker,
Early in the morning?
Hit him with a stick so he topples over,
Bash him with a brick till he's blue all over,
Bury him in the nick and cover him over,
Just as day is dawning."

Well well, if it isn't our Florrie Lampshade.

The DOCTOR comes on.

DOCTOR: Okay, Punch, why don't you tell me about when you were a kid?

PUNCH: Mr Plod been teaching you accents, has he?

LIZ / DOCTOR: Punch, behave yourself. (*as the DOCTOR*) Well, what's the answer?

PUNCH: How about, cos it's none of your business?

DOCTOR: No, but it might help to figure out where you're going.

PUNCH: Back to my cell, at a guess.

DOCTOR: That's quite witty.

PUNCH: Haven't you heard? I'm the prison funny man.

DOCTOR: Which often hides some kind of sadness.

PUNCH: Don't make me fucking laugh.

DOCTOR: Early years critically impact us for the rest of our lives.

PUNCH: You what?

DOCTOR: Don't kid me, Punch. You understand long words. Go back as far as you can remember. To before you went to school. When you were two years old, say.

PUNCH does not respond.

Then I guess I'll have to do some guessing, and I want you to tell me if I'm right. You've learnt to talk, but folk never seem to grasp what you want.

PUNCH: Maybe.

DOCTOR: Tell me about your mother.

PUNCH: Stupid slag.

DOCTOR: She ought to understand you, but she doesn't. You have to scream to get her attention.

Again PUNCH does not respond.

What about when you were older? Did you have many girl friends?

PUNCH: I'm not a poof if that's what you mean.

DOCTOR: Did you hit them?

PUNCH: No. They always rolled over happy as anything and opened wide.

DOCTOR: How did you get on with your father?

PUNCH: What father?

DOCTOR: Did he hit you?

PUNCH: Whenever he left off belting my mother.

DOCTOR: Then he left home?

PUNCH: If you know, why are you asking?

DOCTOR: I need you to tell me. How did you feel when he left?

PUNCH: I felt angry, didn't I?

DOCTOR: Angry he'd gone? Or angry he'd not gone sooner?

PUNCH: Just angry.

DOCTOR: Okay. Let's think about the place where you lived instead.

Pause.

Well?

PUNCH: Quiet! I'm thinking.

DOCTOR: The reason I'm asking is, there's a clear correlation between environmental incivilities and offending behaviour.

PUNCH: Enviro who?

DOCTOR: Graffiti.

PUNCH: I never graffitied. I couldn't climb over the fence.

DOCTOR: But you learnt to be aggressive?

PUNCH: You learn by doing.

DOCTOR: When did you start?

PUNCH: I can't remember.

DOCTOR: In school?

PUNCH: Pass.

DOCTOR: Or at home?

PUNCH: Pass.

DOCTOR: Was it when you got into glue-sniffing, maybe?

PUNCH: No.

DOCTOR: Or perhaps you tried cannabis? Or hallucinogens?

PUNCH: Oh, yes. Nail varnish. Paint stripper. Anything I could get my hands on. I stopped going home, I dropped out of school…

DOCTOR: Did you?

PUNCH: No. I had tea with the vicar every Friday.

DOCTOR: Did the other kids make fun of you?

PUNCH: I'd have thumped them if they did.

DOCTOR: They didn't call you names?

PUNCH: Such as?

DOCTOR: I don't know, Punchbag?

PUNCH: No.

DOCTOR: Or Humpy?

PUNCH: Don't you ever, ever, say that again! Nobody calls me that except Jude, you hear! Nobody!!

DOCTOR: You won't use violence with me, Mr Punch.

PUNCH: Violence is in my genes. If there was a war they'd give me a medal for violence.

DOCTOR: And since there isn't a war, you must learn to control what's in your jeans. Did you move on to cocaine?

PUNCH: No comment.

DOCTOR: Then what? Heroin?

PUNCH: No.

DOCTOR: Are you sure?

PUNCH: (*showing DOCTOR his eyes*) I never took H. See? I never took it. So don't go writing in that report that I did.

DOCTOR: I won't.

PUNCH: I was not some pin cushion who wakes up shaking with his eyeballs pointing backwards.

DOCTOR: Okay, okay.

PUNCH: I never took that funky junk. Never. Cos I'm me, right? Punch. Not some kid you read about in textbooks, wetting the bed cos his father lobs him round the room or so stoned he can't find his arse with both hands.

DOCTOR: Okay, I said.

PUNCH: I've been there, done that…

DOCTOR: Whoa! Stop!

PUNCH: …and I don't want to go back there!

DOCTOR: Stop. Take time out… Stay cool. Okay?

PUNCH: Hm.

DOCTOR: What happened when the horrors of adolescence kicked in?

PUNCH: What with the pimples and the cowpox I never had a chance at all.

The DOCTOR looks at PUNCH.

I caught the pox off this absolute cow in Epping.

DOCTOR: Suppose you wanted an extra helping in the canteen here. How would you set about that?

PUNCH: Get some bloke who's sick to give you his ration.

DOCTOR: And if someone else asked him for it first?

PUNCH: Get the someone else to unask him for it.

DOCTOR: How?

PUNCH: You go down on your knees and say please, nicely.

DOCTOR: And if he refuses?

PUNCH: You kick him in the crutch.

DOCTOR: There's no other way of getting what you want?

PUNCH: Who cares, as long as it works?

DOCTOR: Sure it works. You scream blue blazes when you're a kid, and you go on doing it until one fine day, hey presto! it stops working.

PUNCH: It never stopped working for me.

DOCTOR: Do you think alcohol has anything to do with the kind of aggression we're talking about?

PUNCH: I think, if you'd spent less time with your nose stuck in books and a bit more out there in the real world, you wouldn't have to ask a lot of bloody stupid questions.

DOCTOR: Are the other staff in here stupid as well?

PUNCH: You're glove puppets, the lot of you, someone else's finger up your brains.

DOCTOR: What about your wife?

PUNCH: You leave my Jude out of it!

DOCTOR: Hold it! Hold it! Stay right there.

Pause.

I figure we just identified another anger trigger.

PUNCH: Yes, we bloody did.

DOCTOR: Well, the good news is, there are lots of ways of dealing with anger.

PUNCH: What? Another spell in solitary?

DOCTOR: We'll try Atinogin.[2]

PUNCH: I thought it came in bottles.

DOCTOR: That's pretty close to the truth. It's an alcohol substitute. It makes you feel better about the world.

PUNCH: I don't need it.

DOCTOR: I'll get it prescribed in case. And when I get mad, I like to go for a nice long walk.

PUNCH: Then I hope you choke on your lead.

---

2 *A tin o' gin.*

The DOCTOR goes off.

Because when I get out there'll be bits of bitches stuck to the ceiling. And gobs of slobs running down the walls.

The CHAPLAIN comes on.

Including this one.
(*singing, to the tune of the Christmas carol*)
"While slappers washed their smalls by night
All seated round the tub,
This nice man with the wings came down
And put them in the club."
Hallo, Vicar. Did you know you've got your God collar on back to front?

CHAPLAIN: I worked that out a long time ago: G – O – D, D – O – G. A little bird tells me you're half-way round the board.

PUNCH: I am. And I'm waiting to throw a double.

CHAPLAIN: Are you quite sure you're ready?

PUNCH: Wouldn't you be if you'd been banged up for two years two months and ninety-seven days?

CHAPLAIN: I expect I would.

PUNCH: I couldn't be readier. I've done reading, writing and rithmetic, art, acrobatics and Atinogin, planing, polishing and potato peeling, psychobabble, sibannacs and social skills. And none of it's worked so they've sent you to pray for a miracle.

CHAPLAIN: How are things at home?

PUNCH: The star of the local am dram is screwing the missis as we speak.

CHAPLAIN: What about in here?

PUNCH: Life couldn't be rosier.

CHAPLAIN: Good.

PUNCH: Yeah, I've always wanted to share a shoe-box with a fruitcake who wraps his goolies in newspaper and spends the night farting and sawing at the bars with his teeth.

CHAPLAIN: You know, if you meet us half-way, you'll get a lot more out of being here.

PUNCH: What you mean is lick your arses and keep my nose clean. Which can't be done, when you think about it.

CHAPLAIN: It can if you set your mind to it.

PUNCH: Tried, have you?

CHAPLAIN: You never know what may happen in life if you want something badly enough.

PUNCH: I'll tell you what happens in life. You have a laugh, you get your leg over, and you try not to walk in the shit.

CHAPLAIN: Is that all there is?

PUNCH: We're baboons, every single one of us.
"Give that here."
"I was eating that."
"But I'm bigger. Piss off."

CHAPLAIN: When you look up at the night sky, do you never have the feeling there's more to it than that?

PUNCH: Such as?

CHAPLAIN: Have you never felt there's a candle somewhere in the darkness?

PUNCH: There was a young nun from Strathclyde,
Who tried to light up her inside.
Don't shove it so hard,
Said Sister Bernard,
Gently now, just let it glide.

CHAPLAIN: A symbol of peace, said Sister Bernice.

PUNCH: It helps if you give it a grease. Why do church bells have willies? Dong!

CHAPLAIN: Is everything a joke to you?

PUNCH: If you treated me like a human being instead of a bull with a ring through its nose you'd know the answer to that!

CHAPLAIN: Tell me what happens when you get angry.

PUNCH: Sod off.

CHAPLAIN: Do you feel your fists clenching?

PUNCH: (*becoming agitated*) No.

CHAPLAIN: The back of your neck goes rigid? Your chest starts heaving? Your mind goes blank and your vision blurs, and the world flies straight out of the window?

PUNCH lashes out.

Hold it, hold it. Deep breaths. Hhhhhh-ha. That's it, with me. Hhhhhh-ha, hhhhhh-ha. Hhhhhh-ha.

PUNCH subsides.

I wonder, have you ever tried boxing?

PUNCH: Don't be a bigger fucking dickhead than you are already. It's what landed me in here.

CHAPLAIN: Shadow boxing. It's a good way of getting rid of anger. All you have to do is pretend you're lambasting someone you detest.

PUNCH: That's not difficult. Hooh! Hooh!

CHAPLAIN: You see what I mean? Shall we have a go? Not too close, or you will lose your chance of parole.

PUNCH: Heugh! Heugh!

CHAPLAIN: That's it. Get it off your chest. That's for the temper we cannot contain, for the bile and the spleen and the rage and the pain.

PUNCH: That's for the judge who put me inside. And another for Snipes who lay down and died.

CHAPLAIN: Good. Good.

PUNCH: And several for doctors and teachers and narks, and governors and chaplains and Tobies that barks.

CHAPLAIN: That's it. Excellent. Keep your guard up. Go on, you yellow-belly. Fight me if you dare.

PUNCH: Hey! Where did you learn boxing?

CHAPLAIN: I used to run a boys' club.

PUNCH: Not down by the – ?

CHAPLAIN: Uh-huh. You're not the only one to have put Snipes on the canvas in your time.

PUNCH: Well, I'll be choir-boyed. Then why aren't you in here as well?

CHAPLAIN: Probably because I didn't hit him so hard. Though we all do things we regret.

PUNCH: You certainly do.

CHAPLAIN: I've never choir-boyed anyone, but evil is in each and every one of us. We have to fight the battle every day, because if we let the evil take over, society falls apart. It's not just a question of booking a seat in heaven. It matters in the here and now. And quite often it does help to say a prayer.

PUNCH: Go ahead if it gives you a kick.

CHAPLAIN: I shall. Dear Lord, look with kindness on your servant Punch. As he prepares to go out into the world, give him the courage to choose what is right, to resist what he knows to be wrong, to understand his anger and to overcome it, to love others as you love him, to see the good in his fellow beings and to forgive them their stupidities, and to live and laugh according to your will. And give us all your help to do the same. Now and for ever. Amen.

PUNCH: Finished?

CHAPLAIN: Yes.

PUNCH: (*hitting ROB, kicking and stamping on him with real, vicious violence*) Good. Because that's for the shithead that

knocked off my wife, for the selfish bastard that ruined my life.
LIZ rushes on and pulls PUNCH away.

LIZ: Stop it! Stop. For God's sake. That's not in the fucking script.

PUNCH: So what are you going to do about it? Eh, [Liz]?

PUNCH goes off. ROB gets unsteadily to his feet, obviously hurt. He is helped off by LIZ.

LIZ (*or the* STAGE MANAGER) We'll take the interval there. [Twenty] minutes, ladies and gentlemen.

END OF ACT ONE

ACT TWO

PUNCH comes on, followed by LIZ dressed as the DOCTOR.

PUNCH: Huh. What do you want?

LIZ: To do the second Doctor scene.

PUNCH: Is that why she's wearing the white coat, you reckon, Punch? No, it's so she can tell white lies, Mr P.

LIZ / DOCTOR: Are you ready? Okay? (*As the DOCTOR*) So, like we said, when the anger kicks in, you need to walk away.

PUNCH does not respond.

And sometimes it takes more courage to walk than to confront a problem head on. But now you can do that because we teased out the causes of your anger.

Again PUNCH does not respond.

You were a classic case of behavioural disturbance, impulsivity and aggression caused by peer pressure, poverty, lack of skills development and absence of parental control. But now you've come to terms with the world and you've found your feet.

PUNCH: I found my feet ages ago. In my socks.

DOCTOR: I'm serious. When you showed up here you were blaming Snipes, right? And your ma. And now you recognise that for what it was. Blame shift. Distorted perspectivity.

PUNCH: But now I've been rehabbed. I know where I'm coming from and I can see where I'm going. Yeah, yeah…

DOCTOR: You do. And you know the triggers that can stimulate aggressivity, and how to avoid them.

PUNCH: Like going for a nice long walk.

DOCTOR: Where are you going?

PUNCH: For a nice long walk.

LIZ: (*lapsing back into her natural voice*) Punch, you can't.

PUNCH: Yes, I can. I'm done. I'm sorted. So I'm suspending the suspension of disbelief.

LIZ: Sit down.

PUNCH: No.

LIZ: Sit down!

Pause.

(*in the voice of* JUDY)

Hallo, Punch.

Pause.

You say, "Who are you?"

Pause.

You say, "Who are you?"

PUNCH: No, I don't.

LIZ: What, then?

PUNCH: I say, I'm fleeing the roar of the greasepaint.

LIZ: Oh, for heaven's sake.

PUNCH: You just watch me.

LIZ: Punch…

PUNCH: Because you're not telling me what to do any more.

LIZ: I see. All right.

PUNCH: So you won't mind if I step out of the magic square.

LIZ: I thought we'd got over this kind of thing.

PUNCH: That is what you called it, isn't it? Look at them. They're wondering whether this is in the script. Aren't you? Eh?

LIZ: That's enough, Punch.

PUNCH: It's not, so you can stop wondering.

LIZ: That's enough. Stop it!

PUNCH: If you don't believe me – .

PUNCH goes off.

LIZ: I'm sorry about this, ladies and gentlemen. He's a bit on edge after – well, you saw what happened before the interval but I'm sure we'll – (*to PUNCH*) We need to do the next prison scene.

PUNCH comes back with the DSM's supposed copy of the script, which he passes to the audience.[3]

PUNCH: It's the Chaplain next.

LIZ: Yes, but since you kicked hell out of him...

PUNCH: Have a look. Pass it round. Page [sixty], I think it is.

LIZ: (*in the voice of JUDY*) How are you getting on with your acrobatics, Punch?

PUNCH: She is trying hard, isn't she, our [Liz]? The only problem is, I'm not going to do another prison scene ever again, not here or anywhere, so you can bring up the house lights and give them their money back. Oh no, I forgot. We started the second half, so they don't get it back. Sorry, lippos and stents, but thems is the rules. And we all have to live by rules, like Mr Noddy says.

LIZ: It's only a few more scenes.

PUNCH: Then you do them. You and David fucking Tenant, or whoever he thinks he is.[4]

LIZ: How the hell can we?

PUNCH: Because you're actors!

LIZ: We can't because you've probably broken his ribs. For all I know you've...

PUNCH: (*to the audience*) You don't mind if I sit here, do you?

---

3 *A bogus script showing the "missing" scenes can be supplied by the Author.*

4 *The name of an actor in the news.*

LIZ: …punctured a lu– Will you listen to me for once?

PUNCH: I'm quite looking forward to this. See what a cock-up they make of it.

LIZ: Punch!

PUNCH: What?

LIZ: You wrote this blessed play, remember?

PUNCH: Do you want to borrow my hat? You can have the extra hump if you like.

LIZ: I said, you wrote this play.

PUNCH: No, I didn't.

LIZ: Yes, you did.

PUNCH: You told me to write a play. So I did, and then I said, "What shall we call it?" And you said, "Call it The Prebumptious Mr Punch." "Why?" I said. "Because that's what the story sounds like," you said.

LIZ: We had all this out when you wanted to act in it.

PUNCH: Yes, and what did you do? You and whatsisname, that free-loader who stole my idea, whose name is on the programme…

LIZ: Peter.

PUNCH: Yes, him. Excuse me. (*borrowing a programme from the audience and ripping it up in disgust*) Here it is, Mr Prebumfaced Punch by Peter the Poacher. It's you and him that turned me into a puppet. So you could poke fun at me.

LIZ: If we did change things, we kept close to the truth.

PUNCH: The truth is, they put me away, and some arsehole tried to get into Jude's knickers. End of story.

LIZ: And that's the story we put in the play!

PUNCH: But what about all the other crap? It's bollocks. It was made up for the sake of a laugh.

LIZ: That's what happens when you write a play. You were in education, you did send up the Governor, and you were more than rude to the Chaplain.

PUNCH: Pleasure domes and dabliabs and nuns from Strathclyde?

LIZ: Yes. And you can't say the Doctor wasn't real.

PUNCH: She never said I was suffering from all those ivities.

LIZ: Yes, she did.

PUNCH: When?

LIZ: In the report she wrote about you.

PUNCH: I never saw it.

LIZ: You weren't meant to.

PUNCH: And I wasn't short-sighted either.

LIZ: Yes, you were. You are being now.

PUNCH: All I wanted to go in the Doctor scene was this: "A day in the life of the Hoodlebums Estate. Eight a.m.: rise and shine, for the ten per cent of grafters with a job. Nine a.m.: kids go to school. Nine-oh-one a.m.: they bunk off school." And then you say, Doctor Nightinjail says, "Weren't you afraid of getting caught?" And I say, "Who by?" And you say, "The police." And I say, "What police?"

LIZ: Yes, and then I say, "Somebody must have cared." And you say…

PUNCH: "If they did, they did sod all about us." Point made. Not my fault.

LIZ: Yes, it is, because we have free will.

PUNCH: No, it isn't. It's my upbringing.

LIZ: It's still you who decide to get angry and hit people.

PUNCH: It's society's fault.

LIZ: So it's society's fault you hit [Rob] so hard we have to apologise and do Act Two on our own?

PUNCH: Yes, it is. Because you and he took the structure away.

LIZ: We didn't know it would work out like it has. Now please, can we do some more of the play?

PUNCH: (*to the audience*) Do you want to see any more of this make-believe?

LIZ: It's no good asking them.

PUNCH: Why not?

LIZ: Because they're the audience! How should they know? Come on. Punch. There are still all those jokes to tell. Your jokes. You're a funny man.

PUNCH: Oh no, I'm not.

LIZ: Oh yes, you are.

PUNCH: Shall we do oranges and lemons? This half's yours and that half's mine.

LIZ: You see, you want to, don't you?

PUNCH: No.

LIZ: Yes, you do.

PUNCH: I'm only doing any more if I can tell it how I want.

LIZ: You can tell it any way you like.

PUNCH: Can I?

LIZ: Of course you can. Cross my heart and hope to – No. Could we have the script back? Thank you. Thanks very much.

PUNCH: You're not going to interrupt like you usually do?

LIZ: No. I promise.

PUNCH: Right then. Here, at long last, baldies and curls, is the true story of Mr Punch with his hump and his stick and his funny voice. Because I have got a hump and a stick and a funny voice, and I have always had a hump and a stick and a funny voice, as any of the kids who laughed at me at school could have told you. Not to mention the big nose and the pot belly. Which is why they called me Punch, and why you and everyone else are likely to go on calling me Punch. So, if you're sitting bumfortably, let us begin. Hallo, boys and girls, I can see you've brought your grannies and granddads. Oh, it's your…

LIZ: We've done that already.

PUNCH: And I want to do it again because they're some of the few words I actually wrote. May I go on?

LIZ signals assent.

So, Punch it is. Punch the immigrant.

LIZ: You were born in Dagenham.

PUNCH: Will you shut up? We were all immigrants at one time or another. We're related to the whole of Africa if you go back far enough. Now, for the last time, may I tell it like it is without a swazzle up my arse?

LIZ: Sorry.

PUNCH: I am an immigrant, and my voice is funny because my mother and father arrived on a banana boat and had to learn English from travellers and costermongers. They came from India, via Italy and France, hidden under barrels of wine and nuts and olive oil, and they were smuggled into London, where they sold jellied eels and pints of winkles and mushy peas. Until everyone took them for granted, and thought they'd been there for ever. They became as English as cricket and chicken tikka. They were tough, they had to be, and we still stand up for ourselves today; we don't take any old lip from suits and wigs and uniforms. That's why most people like us. Because we're moral in our old-fashioned way. If one of our kids steps out of line, he feels the back of his father's hand, and if he does it again, he feels the front as well. Same with the mothers. They respect the fathers, and the fathers respect them. But if a woman as much as looks at anyone else, she'll have the lights knocked out of her so that no one will want to look at her ever again. Because that's the way we live. The way we've always lived. By rules, by morals. And deep down, people know in their hearts that what we stand for is right. They know they need rules. Not the "have to understand where they're coming from" crap that you hear nowadays. Your Mr Nod is right about that. The only problem is, he broke the rules himself. And if some bugger tries to put one over on me or takes the piss because I talk funny or look funny, I tend to shove his teeth down his throat. And what do I get for it? Five years. There you are. That is the story of Punch. The bloke with the hump that the other kids laughed at.

LIZ: And that's the play as you wanted it to be?

PUNCH: Yes.

LIZ: It sounds even more like the puppet show than the version we wrote.

PUNCH: No, it doesn't.

LIZ: For a start, you didn't shove Snipes's teeth down his throat because he took the piss.

PUNCH: I didn't shove Snipes or his teeth anywhere.

LIZ: Yes, you did.

PUNCH: I hit a man in a pub, but he was not called Snipes and the pub was not called the Mulberry Bush.

LIZ: And your parents didn't come from India, either. Your mother was from Limehouse, and your father was from

Ireland, or so you claim. Though heaven knows whether it's true.

PUNCH: It's true because it goes with being Punch.

LIZ: You've never told the truth about anything.

PUNCH: Yes, I have. My mother was a stupid slag, and my father did go away.

LIZ: What for? GBH?

PUNCH: For handling so-called stolen goods. And if everyone who did that was put in the can, the theatre would be empty. Isn't that right, Punch? Couldn't be righter, Mr Punch.

LIZ: Will you stop doing that?

PUNCH: What?

LIZ: Pretending you're two people at once.

PUNCH: We're all two people at once. More than two.

LIZ: Not if we want to stay sane.

PUNCH: When you walk into a classroom, who are you?

LIZ: I'm me.

PUNCH: No, you're not. You're not the [Liz] who shared a bed with me until last night.

LIZ: So who am I?

PUNCH: You're [Liz] the Teacher. And when you're up on a wire you're Joey the Clown. And now you're trying to be [Liz] the actor.

LIZ: I'm still [Liz].

PUNCH: Do you tell your students to roll you over on your front? Do you go on about metaphors and similes when you're wearing spangles on your bum?

LIZ: There are different sides to everyone. But I'm still me.

PUNCH: Well, if you can still be you, I can still be me. But wherever I am, and whichever me I think I'm being, people will always say, "Here comes Punch." So, here does come Punch. Not the imaginary Punch, the puppet Punch, the rat-brained laugh-a-minute ho-ho Punch, but the real Punch, who believes in rules and whose parents or grandparents or great-grandparents or great-great-grandparents did come from India in a barrel of nuts. So when they expect me to hit them, I hit them. Not pretend hit, like on a stage, but for real. And when they expect me to shout my mouth off, I shout my mouth off.

LIZ: Is that what you want? To be a man who hits people and shouts his mouth off?

PUNCH: What I want is to be with you. And if I can't do that, I shall go on being Punch.

LIZ: Let me tell you who you really are.

PUNCH: I know who I am.

LIZ: (*referring to the audience*) Then let me tell *them*.

PUNCH: They don't want to hear your crappy ideas…

LIZ: They've heard your version. Now they can hear mine! As Punch just said, the Jo character is me. Or based on me. Because I teach part-time in prisons when I haven't got any acting work or acrobatics. I'd been in this one for six or seven years, ladies and gentlemen, and suddenly here was this young man. He was bright, as you can tell, but he was not the clever, urbane…

PUNCH: Shut that!

LIZ: He was not the clever, urbane, inventive character you've seen in the play.

PUNCH: I said, shut it!

LIZ: Which would never have been written if it had been left up to him.

PUNCH: Yes, it bloody well would.

LIZ: If I hadn't brought in someone else it would have been one long moan about…

PUNCH: It would have been true! Not like the shit that arse-face Peter the…

LIZ: It would have been one long moan about how the world had treated you…

PUNCH: True! Really true!

LIZ: How the world had treated you badly – the sort of gibberish you've just been spouting. I broke the rules for you! The Prison Service rules! Because I was afraid I'd lose you, that you'd drop back into the mess you were in before. Your vocabulary was expanding, your thinking was becoming complex, you were starting to realise there are ways of expressing yourself besides shouting and hitting people. And if you'd been put outside the gate with your bus fare and a bag of old clothes I knew what would happen. That's why I offered you a home when you came out.

PUNCH: You offered me more than that.

LIZ: I did. And you've never understood how far I stuck my neck out.

PUNCH: You've never understood me.

LIZ: I understood you the moment I clapped eyes on you.

PUNCH: No, you didn't. Because you're not Jude.

LIZ: No, I'm a prison educator! And when you came to me in the Education Unit you couldn't read a word. That's what this is all about, isn't it?

PUNCH: I was dyslexic!

LIZ: No, you weren't. You were too fucking idle to learn!

PUNCH: I learnt like fucking Einstein once I got the fucking chance. I did some fucking genius things in the art class.

LIZ: Oh yes: huge hands, twisted faces, bones that had been set wrong.

PUNCH: A real insight, they called it, into my soul.

LIZ: Ah-soul. More distorted perspectivity.

PUNCH: And you got my poems published.

LIZ: In the prison magazine.

PUNCH: Beautiful poems, you said. Sad poems. Coloured poems.

LIZ: They were, but that doesn't mean they were...

PUNCH: So I was clever. I just hadn't been taught.

LIZ: What I'm trying to get through to you, Punch, is that there are an awful lot of clever people in the world, and that you aren't as clever as you think.

PUNCH: Oh no? Listen to this, burps and turps.
"The World is Blue":
"The world is blue.
The land and sea a mushy blue, a pea-blue blue,
Of pea-blue shit, in which I sit.
My head is red, it's cool and red.
A pool of red, a foolish red.
It's full of shit.
But that shit's blue, and so are you.
And you, and you, and you, and you.
And I am red.
I want my head to be red too,
Inside."

LIZ: That one was clever.

PUNCH: You said you'd never seen anyone's face light up with such a smile when I saw it in print. You smiled yourself.

LIZ: Yes, all right. There's no point in arguing about it.

PUNCH: Thank you. So I am clever.

ROB comes on.

Oh, hallo. What did the candle say to the snuffer?

LIZ: Are you fit to carry on?

ROB: They patched me up.

PUNCH: You get on my wick.

ROB: Have you explained?

LIZ: As best I can.

ROB: Where are we?

PUNCH: Shaftesbury Avenue. Nearest tube: Cockfosters.[5]

LIZ: God knows. Are you really okay?

ROB: Yes, I'll get it X-rayed later.

PUNCH: Can we have the lights for Scene Twelve please?

LIZ: No. We'll jump to the second visit scene.

PUNCH: You carry on. Don't mind me.

LIZ: We can't do Scene Twelve.

PUNCH: Yes, you can. It's crap because it was written by Peter the Parasite, but you can still do it.

LIZ: But we're in – .

PUNCH: Yeah. You are, aren't you?

---

5 *The location of the performance with a joke tube or train station.*

LIZ looks at ROB, who shrugs. They become JUDY and the POLICEMAN.

PUNCH goes back to sit with the audience.
Don't look so worried. I shall sit here as quiet as a dead church mouse.

JUDY and the POLICEMAN are in bed in JUDY's house.

JUDY: I remember the first time Punch and me – it put my dad in the shade, I can tell you.

POLICEMAN: Me too, I expect.

JUDY: I didn't mean – .

POLICEMAN: That's all right

JUDY: You're – gentle.

POLICEMAN: I hope that's a compliment.

JUDY: It is. I never knew it could be like that.

POLICEMAN: I'm glad you know now.

JUDY: So am I, cos with Punch it was always – well, you can imagine how it was.

POLICEMAN: Wham bam, thank you mam?

JUDY: Except there wasn't usually a thank you.

POLICEMAN: How did you get yourself mixed up with him?

JUDY: I saw him hitting some kid for laughing at him. And I said, Good for you. I still think Good for you in a funny kind of a way. I shouldn't be saying this.

POLICEMAN: It's all right.

JUDY: I shouldn't. Not when –.

POLICEMAN: You should, because you need to. I don't mind.

JUDY: (*laughing at the memory*) He used to drop round with a bottle and a couple of ratburgers, he called them. And if my mum came home and found us lying on the sofa or the floor or wherever we were, she'd just say, Oh, hallo, and sit down and watch the telly as if nothing was going on. And then when he'd gone again he'd send me lovely text messages. Funny messages. Sometimes ten times a day.

POLICEMAN: You still miss him. Don't you?

JUDY nods.

Nothing wrong with that. It means your heart's in the right place.

JUDY: I knew he'd been inside, but I was helping him get away from all that. And he was, until he got into that fight in the Mulberry. And now I – I don't know what to say to him any more.

POLICEMAN: Part of the penalty, that is, my love.

JUDY: But I don't know what he's going to do without me.

POLICEMAN: You have to think of yourself as well, you know. And the Baby.

JUDY: But he's – well, it's different when you've lived with someone, isn't it? You can't just, sort of, wave goodbye and forget them. Not like my dad who used to come round for his bag of oats and a laugh.

POLICEMAN: A laugh?

JUDY: If he was in one of his moods he'd give me a belt, but not otherwise.

POLICEMAN: I'd never do that.

JUDY: Because you're different. When I got pregnant and they…

POLICEMAN: Punch was the father?

JUDY: Yes! Well, I think he was. No, I'm sure. He must have been. By then. Anyway, when they gave us this flat, I thought it was going to be brilliant. And it was for a bit. But –.

POLICEMAN: Too much like living on a big dipper?

JUDY: Yes.

POLICEMAN: Up one minute and down again the next?

JUDY: You do have a lovely way of putting things.

POLICEMAN: Some women fall for it, see? The swagger, the "Here, look at me," the excess testosterone. But the things he says are only funny if he's got his fist round your windpipe.

JUDY: Only once.

POLICEMAN: What?

JUDY: His hands round my throat. It was only the once.

POLICEMAN: Oh, God – and then I suppose someone just happened along and he dropped back into being Mr Nice Guy?

JUDY: How did you guess?

POLICEMAN: Because I've seen it more times than I can count.

JUDY: He didn't mean to hurt me. Not really.

POLICEMAN: I've heard that a thousand times too. Judy, you've been let down by the men in your life all along the line. And the women.

JUDY: You know what I like about you?

POLICEMAN: Everything, naturally.

JUDY: You keep your truncheon in your trousers – well, you did – and you talk to me as if I've got a brain.

POLICEMAN: You have. As well as a heart. And I don't like to see them abused by men who think women are nothing but totty.

JUDY: You don't think that.

POLICEMAN: I like a nice pair of pins.

JUDY: Oh, you! You've turned my whole world upside down, you have, Owen.

POLICEMAN: Right side up, I should say.

JUDY: It's funny, isn't it?

POLICEMAN: What is?

JUDY: You're a bit like Punch on the quiet.

POLICEMAN: I'm not!

The stage suddenly blacks out.

JUDY: That never used to happen when he was around

POLICEMAN: Probably because he bypassed the meter.

PUNCH: Bravo. Very well done. I'm sure the rest of the run will be a great success.

The lights come up again. PUNCH starts to go off.

LIZ: Punch, wait. If we could manage that, we can manage the second visit scene.

PUNCH: No, we can't.

LIZ: Yes, we can. You needn't act. Just be yourself.

PUNCH: Acting is being?

LIZ: That's right. You remember.

PUNCH: But now I've learnt that being is acting.

LIZ: Then be Punch. Go on. You did your monologue.

PUNCH: Hm.

LIZ: Please. See how we go. All right?

PUNCH: I'll think about it.

PUNCH paces the floor of his cell.

Four hundred and one, four hundred and two, four hundred and nine…

LIZ becomes JUDY.

ROB: Four hundred and three comes next.

PUNCH: Why don't you just fuck off?

ROB makes to hit PUNCH, but thinks better of it and goes off.

JUDY: Hallo, Punch.

PUNCH: Who are you?

LIZ / JUDY: That's it. You'll be fine. (*speaking as JUDY*) You know who I am.

PUNCH: I thought you'd gone to Australia.

JUDY: It's a long way.

PUNCH: It is, isn't it?

JUDY: Three buses it takes me to get here.

PUNCH: Then you'd better start back while there's time. It'd make a good pub in here, wouldn't it, Jude? Little greasy tables. Bars on the windows. Some miserable git in the corner making sure you don't enjoy yourself. Ye Olde Glasshouse. Do not ask for credit.

JUDY: How are you getting on with your acrobatics?

PUNCH: I've been along that tightrope eight times now.

JUDY: That's nice.

PUNCH: It's more than nice. I'll be over the wall soon.

JUDY: They won't let you, will they?

PUNCH: I mean I'm getting out. You and me together again, eh, Jude? Straight down the Mulberry for a pint of Gary Glitter, and then, wahay!

JUDY: You can't go back there.

PUNCH: Why not? Snipes won't be there.

JUDY: That's why you can't!

PUNCH: What's the matter, Jude? Why's the sun gone in? Aren't you pleased I'm coming back to you and Baby?

JUDY: Yes. Course I am.

PUNCH: Who's looking after her?

JUDY: Someone.

PUNCH: That health visitor woman?

JUDY: No. Ginny decided I could manage on my own.

PUNCH: Who, then?

JUDY: Someone.

PUNCH: What someone?

JUDY: Just someone!

PUNCH: I want to know who!

JUDY: Quiet. He's starting to look at us.

PUNCH: Who is in my house looking after my daughter?

JUDY: Look, I've written you this letter, Punch.

PUNCH: What do you mean, you've written me a letter?

JUDY hands over the letter surreptitiously.

JUDY: Don't wave it about. They'll see it.

PUNCH: Why can't you say it to my face?

JUDY: There's no need to get out of your pram.

PUNCH: I am not getting out of my pram.

JUDY: On your high horse, then.

PUNCH: I am not getting on my high horse. I just want to know why you wrote me a letter.

JUDY: Sometimes it's easier.

PUNCH: Not for you, it isn't.

JUDY: Don't be nasty, Punch.

PUNCH: You can't even write your own name.

JUDY: Yes, I can. I've started classes again.

PUNCH: Who put that idea in your little wooden bonce?

JUDY: No one.

PUNCH: If I'd wanted you to read I'd have taught you myself.

JUDY: You didn't though, did you?

PUNCH: What's this letter about then, Shakespeare?

JUDY: Nothing. It's just that —.

PUNCH: What?

JUDY: I've got to be going, Punch. I'll see you next time.

PUNCH: Will you?

JUDY: Goodbye, Punch.

PUNCH: Is that what you're telling me? Goodbye? Just like that? After four years and a baby?

JUDY goes off.

(*opening the letter and reading*) "Dear Punk" – that's a good start – "I have decidded to putt this in writting..." Cos you're too much of a coward to say it out loud. "I thing it wood be bitter if we was to go our own wags. You and me was always..." something or other... "and now im – I'm..." God knows what it says, but we all know what it means. Got bored and hung out the For Sale sign. "So I dont thing there is mush bint in contiki..." Bugger all bint in contiki. "I wood of written sooner only I did not want to worry you." Worry me? Worry me!? "Me and Oven" – I bet he's a gas – "Me and Oven are gonig to try and make a go off it." They lock me up for looking after myself, they play football with my head, and now they let my

Jude run off with a cooker! "Wood you bleep it, he's gong to run a puppy teeter!"

PUNCH casts about for something to hit. LIZ comes on.

LIZ: Easy, Punch. Easy.

PUNCH: He wants to run this one, doesn't he? This fucking puppet theatre.

LIZ: Not here. Please.

PUNCH: He's already got you on a string.

LIZ: Punch, please.

PUNCH: Then tell me why you want to leave me!

LIZ: We can't talk about it now.

PUNCH: Why not? Have you got a class to teach? Or have I got to back to the wing?

LIZ: No.

PUNCH: What, then? Is it time to get the van packed?

LIZ: No.

PUNCH: Or is it because I'm schizoid?

LIZ: *(referring to the audience)* It's because you're embarrassing everyone. That's why.

PUNCH: It's the ivities. That's what it is, isn't it?

LIZ: If you really want an answer, it's because I felt trapped. As if I was in a cage.

PUNCH: It was me in the cage. Four paces this way, three paces that.

LIZ: You crowded me. Like you're doing now.

PUNCH: Because I want to be with you.

LIZ: I could never go anywhere without you wanting to know where and when and who with.

PUNCH: Because I love you. You're the only person I've ever loved. You and Jude.

LIZ: Which is precisely what your problem is.

PUNCH: How can loving someone be a problem?

LIZ: Because you don't understand what love is.

PUNCH: I'm lousy in bed? Is that what you're saying?

LIZ: No. You're a bloody good lover. You are. Your only trouble is, not enough people have told you so.

PUNCH: Oh, sure.

LIZ: We'll sort something out. We'll have to, because we can't have this performance every night. Not in front of an audience.

PUNCH: Why not?

LIZ: Look, Punch. You're a lovely man. You're talented. And I do still love you.

PUNCH: Hah, you so fucking don't.

LIZ: And one day you'll realise there are more kinds of love in the world than you thought. Some of which go a lot deeper than sharing a bed. They do. Really. Come on. Come. Come with me.

LIZ leads PUNCH off.

ROB comes on.

ROB: Well at this point, ladies and gentlemen, Punch is supposed to have a scene with the Prison Governor, but it's only another barrow-load of jokes. "The garden's too shady," "Nothing shady in here," that kind of thing, so it's no loss. But at the end, the Governor has a short soliloquy, in which he says:
I wonder why I work in prisons sometimes. I've been assaulted, I've been spat at, I've seen the same faces time and again, I've seen drugs, alienation, gangs and violence, and I've seen kids in their teens and full-grown men whose lives are in chaos because there's no structure to them. And all the courses and welfare and psychological tests in the world can't put broken lives back together in a lock-up full of social misfits. So often enough, in the dark hours of dawn, I think to myself, why do I bother? But then I remember that sometimes we do put the pieces back together and I plug on, telling myself that I'm part of the solution. Because if I'm not, and there is no solution, there's no point in my being there.

LIZ comes back on.

What's he doing?

LIZ: Sitting with his head in his hands while they find someone to take him back to his digs.

ROB: What do we do now?

LIZ: Be nice to him and hope it turns out better tomorrow, because he's so very nearly there. That's the true tragedy of Mr Punch.

ROB: Why didn't he go back to Judy when he came out?

LIZ: I don't know if there ever was a real Judy. Or a baby.

ROB: Or a policeman?

LIZ: There may have been someone. I've no idea.

ROB: If they do exist and they did what it says in the play – ?

LIZ: That's what I was worried about. It's another of the reasons I gave him a home and – let him share my bed. And he was getting on well. Until – .

ROB: Till you told him it was over between you?

LIZ: Yes. As I'm sure everyone has realised by now.

ROB: It had to happen sooner or later.

LIZ: We should have waited till the end of the run. But that's our problem, not yours, ladies and gentlemen. So, there we are. You've not seen the play we wanted to show you and you'll have an earlier night than you expected, but we hope you don't feel you've had an entirely wasted evening.

ROB: We could still do the final scene.

LIZ: Not without Punch, we can't.

ROB: Yes, we can.

LIZ: How?

ROB: I can play him.

LIZ: You don't know it.

ROB: I've seen it often enough, and it scarcely matters if I balls it up. The whole show's on its arse anyway.

LIZ: That's true.

ROB: So, do we go for it?

LIZ: All right. But you have to understand, ladies and gentlemen, that although the rest of the play bears some relation to reality – well, quite a lot, actually – Punch hadn't a clue how to finish it. So the last scene is pure seaside fantasy and was written by Peter.

ROB: Here we are then. My lords, ladies and jelly-beans: scene the last, in which – you can guess what happens.

ROB goes off. LIZ becomes JUDY and begins talking to the Baby, now two and a half years old.

JUDY: You are a sleepy-head today, Baby. You'd better have a snoozle-wooze. And I must make your Uncle Owen his extra-special tea. Cos today's the big day. The one we've all been waiting for. From now on he's going to be living with us all the time. And you know what I'm going to tell him, don't you, Baby? I'm going to tell him, I'm going to tell him you're going to have a little baby sister. Ooh-ooh-ooh-ooh! I feel all tingly-jingly inside. Isn't that exciting, Baby? Unless your sister's a brother.

The sound of a key in the lock

Oh dear, Baby. Here he is already. He must have got off early. Ooooooh! (*excitement*)

ROB comes in as PUNCH.

ROB / PUNCH: Hallo, my guilty-pie.

JUDY: Punch!

ROB / PUNCH: No, I'm the man from the welfare.

JUDY: I didn't know you'd be out that quick.

ROB / PUNCH: Got off early for good behaviour.

JUDY: I don't believe you.

ROB / PUNCH: Good behaviour in prison, bad behaviour at home.

JUDY: You'd better go all the same.

ROB / PUNCH: I'm as sane as the next bloke nowadays.

JUDY: That's not much comfort.

ROB / PUNCH: I've been reconned. Trained.

JUDY: Then you'd better play trains somewhere else because Owen'll be here soon.

ROB / PUNCH: Oh yes, Oven mark two. This all his idea, is it? Net curtains, tablecloth, serve-you-rights.[6] Very tasteful.

---

6 *Serviettes.*

JUDY: He's been doing a show with his puppet theatre.

ROB / PUNCH: What's it called? "Punk gets stuffed?"

JUDY: It's called "Owen and Judy Live Happily Ever After."

ROB / PUNCH: Only because you've joined *them*. That's what you've done, you've gone blue like all the rest. Mr and Mrs Glove Puppet, with Little Miss Muffet their daughter.

JUDY: Don't come any nearer, Punch.

ROB / PUNCH: How is our darling Baby-boo?

JUDY: She's not yours any more.

ROB / PUNCH: Not mine? But now I've come home, to Baby and you. Out on the town, zippety-doo. Is she still going to be a teacher lady?

JUDY: A health visitor. That's what I want her to be.

ROB / PUNCH: Oh, very nice. Very classy. A real move up the social scale. Is that why you don't want me to be her dad any longer? Your daddy was a hero in shining armour who had to go away to fight dragons. Is that what you tell her? Or maybe he was a one-night stand with a being from outer space. Or a shower of gold that descended out of the clouds. In fact it doesn't matter a jerbil's fart who your daddy was as long as he was anyone but the bloke I lived with, who took me places, who bought me things, who danced with me, who slept with me, who made me laugh. Who loved me. And who thought I loved him. Only now we don't need him any more because we've got the self-cleaning Oven, with his big hairy hotplates and his big hairy knob. Oh yes, I can see your point. You've only got to look at her, with her neat curly wurls and her rosy ruby lips.

JUDY: You've been learning lots of words in prison, then.

ROB / PUNCH: I learnt all sorts of things in prison. Like distorted perspectivity.

JUDY: I thought I heard Owen's car.

ROB / PUNCH: That means when someone pulls the wool over your eyes.

JUDY: He'll be here any minute.

ROB / PUNCH: Your mother and me, we tossed you in the air and you loved every minute of it. Now someone else is tossing you, tossing your mother as well. Cos do you know what your mummy did when your daddy was in prison? That's right, you do, don't you, Baby?

The door-bell rings: bing-bong.

I think you must have heard Owen's car. So what are we going to do about that then? I tell you what. I'll pick you up by the heels and —.

JUDY: No!

ROB / PUNCH: But we could never do that. No, we could never do that.

Bing-bong.

Aren't you going to answer it? I wonder, did your mummy give you your nice hot bath? I'll bet she didn't. Too busy making delicious din-dins. Shall we give you your bath, my little duck? Would you like that? Like a lobster, a bright red lobster singing in its bubble bath? No, we could never do that either.

Bing-bong, bing-bong.

Hasn't Policeman Plod got a key?

JUDY: He must have forgotten it.

ROB / PUNCH: Then you'd better let him in. (*seizing the Baby*) It's all right. I told you I was safe. I'll leave her sleeping peacefully with her little chest going up and down, and a stray hair or two over her face, dreaming of princes and puppy dogs. And I'll tip-toe out the back door and never be heard of again. Cos that's what you want, isn't it?

Bing-bong, bing-bong, bing-bong.

Or then again, I might give her one more toss.
(*singing*) "Rock-a-bye baby, in the tree-top,
When the wind blows, the cradle will rock.
When the bough breaks, the cradle will fall..."
Difficult, isn't it? Do I grab my baby – my baby, not his, because she's not his any more – or do I make a run for the door and let in Sir Gas-hob? Quite a dilemma, isn't it? I wouldn't like to be in your Mummy's shoes, Baby. Not for all the tea she never offered me. Oh, whatever shall I do?

JUDY makes a dash for the door – too late. ROB / PUNCH throws the Baby head first to the floor.

Oh dear, I've dropped the baby.

JUDY screams. ROB / PUNCH treads the Baby into the floor.

That's the way to do it. That's the way to do it...

JUDY runs to the Baby. ROB strikes her to the ground and kicks her repeatedly. Eventually he stops, and looks aghast at what he has done.

PUNCH comes on and slowly takes in the scene.

PUNCH: Oh, yes. That is the way to do it.

ROB: What now?

PUNCH: The punters go home.

ROB: What about tomorrow?

PUNCH: Who gives a fuck about tomorrow?

END

www.ingramcontent.com/pod-product-compliance
Lightning Source LLC
Chambersburg PA
CBHW072202100426
42738CB00011BA/2503